CW00530163

LMH OFFICIAL DICTIONARY

OF WEST INDIES CRICKET GROUNDS

Compiled by
L. Mike Henry

In the preparation of this work, we used as reference, Test Cricket Grounds: The complete guide to the world's Test cricket grounds by John Woods.

Cover Design by:Sanya Dockery
Edited by: L. M. Henry
Book Design, Layout & Typesetting by: Sanya Dockery
Photographs taken from http://www.cricketworldcup.com

Currently seeking permission to use the pictures of architectural drawings of newly refurbished and renovated grounds.

Published by: LMH Publishing Limited
7 Norman Road,
LOJ Industrial Complex
Building 10
Kingston C.S.O., Jamaica
Tel: 876-938-0005; 938-0712
Fax: 876-759-8752
Email: lmhbookpublishing@cwjamaica.com
Website: www.lmhpublishing.com

Printed in China   ISBN 13: 978-976-8202-26-0

CONTENTS

Henry, *Mike*

LMH Official Dictionary of West Indies Cricket Grounds

ISBN 978-976-8202-26-0 hardback

Errata

p. 45 *for* RESULTS AT SABINA PARK
   read RESULTS AT ANTIGUA
      RECREATION GROUND

p. 59 *for* RESULTS AT BEAUSEJOUR STADIUM
   read RESULTS AT ANTIGUA
      RECREATION GROUND

p. 66 *for* RESULTS AT ARNOS VALE *read*
      RESULTS AT ANTIGUA RECREATION
      GROUND

P. 76 *for* RESULTS AT QUEENS PARK OVAL
   read RESULTS AT ANTIGUA
      RECREATION GROUND

INTRODUCTION

IN 1930, TEST CRICKET ARRIVED IN THE
Caribbean when England visited for a four match series.

The first encounter (was) on the 11th January at Kensington Oval in Bridgetown, Barbados and the second at Queens Park Oval in Trinidad. Some three weeks later, on the 21st February, the third Test was played in Georgetown at the Bourda Ground, and the final test in April at Sabina Park, Jamaica.

The tour, as would be expected in the days of sea transport, lasted over four months and indeed the English team had to end the match in Jamaica in a draw so that they could catch their boat home. As recorded, the Jamaica match lasted over nine days.

The series ended in a tie with two draws in Barbados and Jamaica and a victory for the West Indies in Guyana.

Since then, the West Indies have added as Test grounds, the Recreation Ground, St Johns, Antigua (1981), Arnos Vale in St. Vincent (1997), the Queens Park Stadium in Grenada (2002) and the Beausejour Stadium in St. Lucia (2003).

For the ICC World Cup 2007, the West Indies have expanded all Test grounds that previously existed, and added the new Greenfields Ground in Trelawny, Jamaica and the Brian Lara Ground in Trinidad, which incidentally, will not be ready in time for the World Cup.

ANTIGUA

ANTIGUA WAS THE HOME OF THE SIBONEYS

(an Arawak descended tribe) from as early as 2000BC.

When Columbus happened on the island in 1493 he claimed it to be Spain's, naming it Santa Maria La Antigua. The Spaniards subsequently lost the island to Great Britain in 1623, and they the British peopled it, 9 years later in 1632.

In 1684, Sir Christopher Coddrington set up the first sugar plantation, using the neighbouring island of Barbuda as a base to provide the provisions for the imported slaves, who were used to clear the forest for the sugar plantations.

History records the sojourn for three (3) years of Horatio Nelson when he developed the Naval facilities in the south of the island. Nelson's dislike for the country was well recorded and is reflected in him calling Antigua 'a dreadful hole'. So much for Nelson's appreciation of beauty. Antigua is the largest of the British Leeward Islands and forms part of the North East Caribbean.

St. Johns is the capital of this twin Island State (now Antigua & Barbuda) and holds a population of some thirty thousand (30,000), representing some 50% of the island's sixty seven thousand (67,000) plus people.

Partly coral, and volcanic; the long reef off the coast protects the long coastline, which now forms the main economic strength of the country, as this is where the centre of tourism exists and where the nearly one million visitors reside in their annual pilgrimage to the sun.

The capital boasts a Cathedral which imposes its presence on the city's skyline and remembers the Colonial past which is evident in this **quaint** city.

Visitors never fail to be impressed by the Antigua & Barbuda museum which unfolds the story of the island with its exhibits of tools, and artifacts of the Arawaks. Cricket lovers can see the bat Sir Vivian Richards used when scoring the fastest Test century ever at the Antigua Recreation Ground.

During a walk through the city, one can visit the Anglican Cathedral St. Johns, Fort James, The Cennotaph, The Court House and the VC Bird monument, visits to which are always rewarding.

Leaving the city, one can enjoy the English Harbour on the South East where Nelson's Dockyard owns Pride of Place – built in the 18th century, it was used to protect the island.

A visit to Shirley's Heights not only exposes one to a Fort, but to a new modern location of entertainment, where on Sundays the Steel and Reggae Bands hold sway. What more could one ask for from a 40 minute drive from the city?

To culminate these attractions, and if your team is not doing as well as you wish, then take a cruise around the island and swim and snorkel away your cares in the shallow waters of Paradise Reef, and close off the trip with Beach Cricket on one of the 365 beaches.

ARC ANTIGUA RECREATION GROUND

Stadium capacity 1,200 persons. The Antigua Recreation Ground is home to the Leeward Island Cricket Association, becoming the 5th Test venue in the W.I. in 1981 during England's tour of that year.

Now renowned for the exploits of Brian Lara, in 1994 and 2004 when he scored, 365 and 400 respectively (still world records today). A batsman's paradise, in paradise, this is the ground where W.I. scored 418 to beat Australia in 2003, another World Record. Batting last, the West Indies achieved this milestone, considered then to be unattainable.

Vivian Richards has chipped in with 3 centuries on the ground, one off 56 balls in 81 minutes in 1986. That century is the fastest century in the least number of balls received. Four batsmen have several Test centuries in less time but none in fewer balls.

Wassim Akrams (11 wickets for 110 runs) in Pakistan's defeat here in 2000, is the best performing bowler on this ground.

As you depart to the CV Bird Airport, (8km) from the country, you will wave goodbye to one of the finest islands in the Caribbean.

STATISTICS

WIN/LOSS RECORD

Country	Played	Won	Drawn	Lost	Tie
South Africa	1	1	-	-	-
West Indies	19	7	9	3	-
India	3	-	3	-	-
New Zealand	1	-	1	-	-
Australia	5	2	1	2	-
Pakistan	2	-	1	1	-
England	6	-	3	3	-
Sri Lanka	1	-	-	1	-

HIGHEST INDIVIDUAL AGGREGATES
(West Indies Unless stated)

Player	Mat	Inn	NO	Runs	Ave	HS	50	100
Brian Lara	12	19	1	1628	90.44	400	6	4
Desmond Haynes	7	10	1	733	81.44	167	3	3
Carl Hooper	10	15	4	656	59.64	178	0	3
Shiv Chanderpaul	8	12	2	570	57.00	136	2	2
Viv Richards	6	8	1	433	61.86	178	0	3
Gordon Greenidge	6	7	1	429	71.50	154	1	2
Jimmy Adams	5	9	3	424	70.67	208	2	1
Richie Richardson	6	10	0	378	37.80	154	1	1
Ramnaresh Sarwan	5	8	0	337	42.13	105	2	1
Justin Langer(Aus)	2	4	0	331	82.75	127	1	2

TOP WICKET TAKERS
(West Indies Unless stated)

Player	Mat	Bll	Md	Runs	Wkt	Ave	BB	S/R
Curtly Ambrose	11	2328	109	945	48	19.69	5/37	48.50
Courtney Walsh	12	3032	102	1250	45	27.78	6/54	67.38
Malcolm Marshall	4	937	35	438	19	23.05	4/87	49.32
Ian Bishop	4	682	21	355	15	23.67	5/84	45.47
Wasim Akram (Pak)	2	556	26	248	13	19.08	6/61	42.77
Joel Garner	3	651	22	279	13	21.46	5/63	50.08
Mervyn Dillon	3	701	23	331	12	27.58	4/112	58.42
Carl Hooper	10	1456	58	620	11	56.36	3/69	132.36
Glenn McGrath (Aus)	3	788	47	287	10	28.70	3/50	78.80
Waqar Younis (Pak)	2	426	13	207	10	20.70	5/104	42.60

HIGHEST INDIVIDUAL SCORES
(West Indies Unless stated)

400	Brian Lara	v	England 2003-04
375	Brian Lara	v	England 1993-94
208	Jimmy Adams	v	New Zealand 1995-96
178	Viv Richards	v	Australia 1983-84
178	Viv Richards	v	Pakistan 1983-84
177	Matthew Hayden (Aus)	v	2002-03
175	Robin Smith (Eng)	v	1993-94
167	Desmond Haynes	v	England 1989-90
154	Gordon Greenidge	v	India 1982-83
154	Richie Richardson	v	Australia 1983-84

BEST INDIVIDUAL BOWLING PERFORMANCES
(West Indies Unless stated)

19.1-3-78-7	Jermaine Lawson	v	Australia 2002-03
21.3-7-54-6	Courtney Walsh	v	Australia 1994-95
26.2-7-61 -6	Wasim Akram (Pak)	v	1999-00
25-5-74-6	Colin Croft	v	England 1980-81
23.4-13-34-5	Muttiah Muralitharan (SL)	v	1996-97
13.1 -3-37-5	Curtly Ambrose	v	Sri Lanka 1996-97
30-12-49-5	Wasim Akram (Pak)	v	1999-00
20-2-61 -5	Danny Morrison (NZ)	v	1995-96
20.5-2-63-5	Joel Garner	v	Australia 1983-84
32-12-68-5	Curtly Ambrose	v	New Zealand 1995-96

HIGHEST PARTNERSHIPS (West Indies Unless stated)

Wkt	Runs	Batsmen	Match
1st	298	Gordon Greenidge & Desmond Haynes (WI)	1989-1 990 v England
2nd	200	Aunshuman Gaekwad & Mohinder Amarnath (Ind)	1982-1983
3rd	308	Richie Richardson & Viv Richards (WI)	1983-1984 v Australia
4th	183	Brian Lara & Keith Arthurton (WI)	1993-1994 v England
5th	219	Brian Lara & Shiv Chanderpaul (WI)	1993-1 994 v England
6th	282	Brian Lara & Ridley Jacobs (WI)	2003-2004 v England
7th	217	VVS Laxman & Ajay Ratra (Ind)	2001-2002
8th	110	Lee Germon & Dipak Patel (NZ)	1995-1996
9th	96	Inzamam-Ul-Haq & Nadeem Khan (Pak)	1992-1993
10th	106	Carl Hooper & Courtney Walsh (WI)	1992-1993 v Pakistan

RESULTS AT ANTIGUA RECREATION GROUND

Date	Countries	Result
27/03/1981	v England	drawn
28/04/1983	v India	drawn
07/04/1984	v Australia	won by an innings and 36 runs
11/04/1986	v England	won by 240 runs
12/04/1990	v England	won by an innings and 32 runs
27/04/1991	v Australia	lost by 157 runs
01/05/1993	v Pakistan	drawn
16/04/1994	v England	drawn
08/04/1995	v Australia	drawn
27/04/1996	v New Zealand	drawn
04/04/1997	v India	drawn
13/06/1997	v Sri Lanka	won by 6 wickets
21/03/1 998	v England	won by an innings and 52 runs
03/04/1999	v Australia	lost by 176 runs
25/05/2 000	v Pakistan	won by 1 wicket
06/04/2001	v South Africa	lost by 82 runs
10/05/2002	v India	drawn
09/05/2003	v Australia	won by 3 wickets
10/04/2004	v England	drawn

BARBADOS

WHEN ONE ARRIVES AT THE GRANTLY ADAMS
International Airport some 17km from the capital Bridgetown, one immediately feels that this a country of order and serenity; living up to its reputation of being "Little England".

The capital lies in Carlisle Bay in the South West corner of the island, housing some 130,000 houses, almost half the population of the country.

Being the most Easterly of the Caribbean, Barbados is often referred to as the gateway to the West Indies.

Formed from erupted volcanoes and surrounded by coral reefs, the island saw its first inhabitants – the Amerindians from Venezuela, all but disappear over the years.

John Powell claimed the island for Britain in 1625 and by 1627 the British had settled at Holestown. Continuous arrivals of settlers, namely small farmers continued, but with the advent of sugar they were squeezed out and by 1650 many returned to England.

The use of slave labour to match the growth of the sugar crop came to an end in 1834 but was followed by indenture labour from India to supplant the freeing of the slave.

In 1966, Barbados became independent and has since developed a vibrant economy based on the still important sugar crop plus Tourism, which is growing constantly due to the beautiful beaches and travel facilities.

The capital has a great deal of colonial charm about it and the Neo-gothic Parliament Buildings, the Law Courts, The Library and the Bridgetown Synagogue, all are worth a visit.

Walking in Barbados/Bridgetown is an acceptable past time allowing one to enjoy the Barbados Museum at the Garisson, National Heroes Square (formally Trafalgar Square), Independence Arch, and the Carenage, with its fine cafés and restaurants, or continue on to the Garrisson Savannah where horse racing takes place.

With an all but unbeatable year round mild tropical climate with 8-9 hours of sunshine daily; one only needs light weight cotton apparel to head for the beach and to enjoy the sun, the sand, the clubs and the restaurants. So whether it be in St. James, Holestown, Spieghtstown or St. Lawrence Gap in the

south, the visitor is never far from the local cuisine and the native specialty of Flying Fish, or Lobster.

The clear turquoise sea moves from the calm of the West Coast (through) to the medium waves at Rockley, and on to the ideal surfing area of the East Coast where the 'waves of Bathsheba' overlay the strong Atlantic currents, sometimes quite dangerous for swimmers.

<u>KENSINGTON OVAL</u>

Home of the Pick Wick Cricket Club since 1882, the ground has the honour to have hosted the first Test held in the West Indies (1930).

This was a high scoring draw with Clifford Roach becoming the first West Indian to score a Test century (122 runs). This was matched by George Headley's 176 in the second innings.

The ground all but oozes the passion the Barbadians have for the game and compliments this with a spate of stands all cherishing the memory of those who have achieved in the name of West Indies Cricket.

The Sir Garfield Sobers Pavilion with the Pick Wick Pavilion houses the players dressing rooms, the George Challenor Stand - the oldest - stands to the left, and houses the VIP area with photographic memorabilia of the past. Next is the three W's Stand (Walcott Weekes, Worrell) which is crouched next to the Greenidge/Haynes stands, and are all complemented by a commercial set of stands which leads to the Joel Garner end of the ground.

Once esconced in the stand of your choice you can relieve the memory of the 1955 feat of the two Barbadians, Dennis Atkinson (219) and Clairemente Depeiza (122) who put on a record 347 for the seventh wicket partnership to save the game for the West Indies; you may also revel in the longest Test innings, when Hanif Mohammed made 337 in 16 hours and 10 minutes.

In 1960, Gary Sobers (286) Frank Worrell (197) reminiscent of Atkinson and Depeiza, shared in a 399 run partnership vs England. This was followed in 1965 by the double Test hundreds by each player (Bill Lawry and Bobby Simpson) when these two Australians became the only openers in Test history, to both score double centuries. And if all of this is not enough, then close your eyes and conjure up Lawrence Rowe's innings of 302 in 16 and a half hours which is still talked about and considered to be the greatest innings the oval has seen, and one which is cherished by the cricket loving Barbadians.

STATISTICS

WIN/LOSS RECORD

Country	Played	Won	Drawn	Lost	Tie
West Indies	4 1	20	15	6	-
England	13	3	6	4	-
Australia	9	2	3	4	-
New Zealand	4	1	1	2	-
Pakistan	5	-	3	2	-
South Africa	2	-	1	1	-
India	8	-	1	7	-

HIGHEST INDIVIDUAL AGGREGATES
(West Indies Unless stated)

Player	Mat	Inn	NO	Runs	Ave	HS	50	100
Desmond Haynes	12	25	5	1210	60.50	145	6	4
Brian Lara	13	23	2	972	46.29	153	7	1
Viv Richards	12	17	1	959	59.94	182	5	3
Garry Sobers	9	14	2	914	76.17	226	3	3
Richie Richardson	11	18	1	882	51.88	160	4	2
Clive Lloyd	9	13	1	807	67.25	157	3	4
Gordon Greenidge	11	21	4	757	44.53	226	3	2
Shiv Chanderpaul	9	16	4	601	50.08	137	3	2
Rohan Kanhai	8	12	1	546	49.64	129	2	2
Clyde Walcott	5	9	1	534	66.75	220	2	1

TOP WICKET TAKERS
(West Indies Unless stated)

Player	Mat	Bll	Md	Runs	Wkt	Ave	BB	S/R
Courtney Walsh	12	3024	114	1342	53	25.32	5/22	57.06
Curtly Ambrose	13	3399	155	1421	52	27.33	8/45	65.37
Malcolm Marshall	8	1812	46	911	49	18.59	7/80	36.98
Joel Garner	7	1486	66	762	31	24.58	4/56	47.94
Andy Roberts	6	1394	49	692	28	24.71	4/31	49.79
Ian Bishop	6	1298	49	628	26	24.15	6/87	49.92
Michael Holding	6	1014	53	445	25	17.80	4/24	40.56
Lance Gibbs	5	1991	124	655	22	29.77	8/38	90.50
Carl Hopper	10	1578	61	632	19	33.26	5/80	83.05
Colin Croft	3	675	19	336	19	17.68	4/39	35.53

HIGHEST INDIVIDUAL SCORES
(West Indies Unless stated)

337	Hanif Mohammad (Pak)		1957-58
302	Lawrence Rowe	v	England 1973-74
226	Garry Sobers	v	England 1959-60
226	Gordon Greenidge	v	Australia 1990-91
220	Clyde Walcott	v	England 1953-54
219	Denis Atkinson	v	Australia 1954-55
210	Bill Lawry (Aus)		1964-65
208	Sherwin Campbell	v	New Zealand 1995-96
201	Seymour Nurse	v	Australia 1964-65
201	Bob Simpson (Aus)		1964-65

BEST INDIVIDUAL BOWLING PERFORMANCES
(West Indies Unless stated)

53.3-37-38-8	Lance Gibbs	v	India 1961-62
22.4-10-45-8	Curtly Ambrose	v	England 1989-90
28.5-7-75 -8	Angus Fraser (Eng)	v	1993-94
20.3-6-74-7	Bruce Taylor (NZ)	v	1971-72
25.3-6-80-7	Malcolm Marshall	v	New Zealand1984-85
37-9-103-7	Jim Laker (Eng)	v	1947-48
24.4-7-34-6	Curtly Ambrose	v	South Africa 1991-92
36-17-67-6	Jacques Kallis (SA)	v	2000-01
30.4-8-76-6	Pedro Collins	v	New Zealand 2002
13-1-77-6	Jeff Thomson (Aus)	v	1977-78

HIGHEST PARTNERSHIPS (West Indies Unless stated)

Wkt	Runs	Batsmen	Match
1st	382	Bill Lawry & Bob Simpson (Aus)	1964-65
2nd	249	Alvin Kallicharran & Lawrence Rowe (WI)	1973-74 v England
3rd	220	Alvin Kallicharran & Viv Richards (WI)	1975-76 v India
4th	399	Garry Sobers & Frank Worrell (WI)	1959-60 v England
5th	281	Steve Waugh & Ricky Ponting (Aus)	1998-99
6th	254	Charlie Davis & Garry Sobers (WI)	1971-72 v New Zealand
7th	347	Denis Atkinson & C Depeiza (WI)	1954-55 v Australia
8th	84	Arshad Ayub & Sanjay Manjrekar (Ind)	1988-89
9th	132	Shaun Pollock & Alan Donald (SA)	2000-01
10th	133	Wasim Bari & Wasim Raja (Pak)	1976-77

RESULTS AT KENSINGTON OVAL

Date	Countries	Result
11/01/1930	v England	drawn
08/01/1935	v England	lost by 4 wickets
21/01/1948	v England	drawn
07/02/1953	v India	won by 142 runs
06/02/1954	v England	won by 181 runs
14/05/1955	v Australia	drawn
17/01/1958	v Pakistan	drawn
06/01/1960	v England	drawn
23/03/1962	v India	won by an innings and 30 runs
05/05/1965	v Australia	drawn
29/02/1968	v England	drawn
01/04/1971	v India	drawn
23/03/1972	v New Zealand	drawn
09/03/1973	v Australia	drawn
06/03/1974	v England	drawn
10/03/1976	v India	won by an innings and 97 runs
18/02/1977	v Pakistan	drawn
17/03/1978	v Australia	won by 9 wickets
13/03/1981	v England	won by 298 runs
15/04/1983	v India	won by 10 wickets
30/03/1984	v Australia	won by 10 wickets
26/04/1985	v New Zealand	won by 10 wickets
21/03/1986	v England	won by an innings and 30 runs
22/04/1988	v Pakistan	won by 2 wickets
07/04/1989	v India	won by 8 runs
05/04/1990	v England	won by 164 runs
19/04/1991	v Australia	won by 343 runs
18/04/1992	v South Africa	won by 52 runs
23/04/1993	v Pakistan	won by 10 wickets
08/04/1994	v England	lost by 208 runs
31/04/1994	v Australia	lost by 10 wickets
19/04/1996	v New Zealand	won by 10 wickets
27/03/1 997	v India	won by 38 runs

3Ws OVAL

Capacity - 4000
Brand new state of the art venue.
Built specifically for World Cup 2007 (warm up matches)

The Three Ws Oval is named after legendary Caribbean cricketers Sir Frank Worrell, Sir Everton Weekes and Sir Clyde Walcott. It is benefiting from a major facelift ahead of the 2007 World Cup, when it hosts four warm-up matches.

GRENADA

SITUATED NORTH OF VENEZUELA, THE ISLAND
lies in the South East Caribbean and is the most southern of
the Windward Islands.

Grenada is known as the spice island and is the second
largest producer of nutmeg in the world.

Grenada boasts a population of some 106,000 of which
some eight to ten thousand live in the capital St. Georges, a
prime example of fine Georgian Architecture and one of the
most scenic cities in the Caribbean.

Like many of its cousins, the island was fought for by the
Spanish, the French and the British, and after some 300 years
it was ceded in 1783 to Britain by the treaty of Versailles.
Grenada remained under British rule until 1967, and gained
its Independence in 1974.

Some nine years later, the over-throw of the Maurice
Bishop Government, led to the invasion of the island by the
USA and the OECS, as the fear of Cuba and Castro's hege-
mony angered the USA.

St. George, a quaint and charming little city, with its
bustling market, boasts a National Museum on Young Street
which is set in on old Army Barracks that was built in 1704.
Park House, the seat of Parliament and the Supreme Court
are attractive buildings to visit. The city is complemented by
fine religious buildings, of which Church Street Methodist
Church (1820) the Anglican Church (1825) and The Catholic
Cathedral (1854) are all prime examples.

Bay Gardens, on the outskirts of the city, is set on the site of an old sugar mill with beautifully laid out gardens, and offers a calm and tranquil respite for the visitor.

It always impresses the visitor when he learns that this country of only 200 sq.km can offer all the above attractions plus magnificent rain forests with Lake Antoine in St. David with its wide array of Flora and Fauna, and La Sagiesse on the South West Coast with its excellent Bird Watching sanctuary.

The island, as expected, boasts a number of glorious beaches for swimming, diving and snorkeling, and Grand Anse is the area of quickest attraction for the visitor who

seeks this escape. Most visitors are content at night to share the conviviality of a quiet drink complemented by the soft sound of the waves and the exciting beat of the Steel Pan.

NATIONAL CRICKET STADIUM

The National Cricket Stadium, formerly known as The New Queens Park Oval, was the seventh ground of the islands to host Test cricket, when New Zealand visited on the 28th June 2002.

Surrounded by hills which are dotted by wooden houses the setting all but has matched the run feast offered by that

first Test - 373 to New Zealand and 470 to the West Indies. In that match Scott Styris hit 107 and Cris Gayle stroked a glorious 204 – Pedro Collins came into his own with 4/66.

Located within five minutes walking distance of the centre of the city, it is all but impossible for the atmosphere of the city not to breathe cricket.

The Players Pavilion is at the Northern end and incorporates the media centre, with the uncovered bleachers on the South and East side, and they form the happiest place to be, as the party-happy locals relax and enjoy their favourite game, and their favourite local rum.

I guess one could only describe the atmosphere at this ground as unique, and the vendors who move through the crowds add their fair share to the day's play.

STATISTICS

WIN/LOSS RECORD

Country	Played	Won	Drawn	Lost	Tie
New Zealand	1	-	1	-	-
West Indies	1	-	1	-	-

HIGHEST INDIVIDUAL AGGREGATES
(West Indies Unless stated)

Player	Mat	Inn	NO	Runs	Ave	HS	50	100
Chris Gayle	1	1	0	204	204.00	204	0	1
Scott Styris (NZ)	1	2	1	176	176.00	107	1	1
Mark Richardson (NZ)	1	2	0	166	83.00	95	2	0
Lou Vincent (NZ)	1	2	0	78	39.00	54	1	0
Nathan Astle (NZ)	1	2	0	69	34.50	69	1	0

TOP WICKET TAKERS (West Indies unless stated)

Player	Mat	Bll	Md	Runs	Wkt	Ave	BB	S/R
Shane Bond (NZ)	1	181	7	104	5	20.80	5/104	36.20
Pedro Collins	1	282	16	96	4	24.00	4/68	70.50
Carl Hooper	1	354	13	110	4	27.50	2/44	88.50
Scott Styris (NZ)	1	150	3	88	2	44.00	2/88	75.00
Cameron Cuffy	1	270	15	96	2	48.00	2/76	135.00

HIGHEST INDIVIDUAL SCORES
(West Indies Unless stated)

204	Chris Gayle	2002
107	Scott Styris (NZ)	2002
95	Mark Richardson (NZ)	2002
71	Mark Richardson (NZ)	2002
69	Nathan Astle (NZ)	2002

BEST INDIVIDUAL BOWLING PERFORMANCES
(West Indies Unless stated)

30.1-7-104-5	Shane Bond (NZ)	2002
30-9-68-4	Pedro Collins	2002
25-3-44-2	Carl Hooper	2002
34-10-66-2	Carl Hooper	2002
42-16-75-2	Mahendra Nagamootoo	2002

HIGHEST PARTNERSHIPS (West Indies Unless stated)

Wkt	Runs	Batsmen	Match
1st	117	Mark Richardson & Lou Vincent (NZ)	2002
2nd	100	Chris Gayle & Ramnaresh Sarwan	2002
3rd	76	Chris Gayle & Brain Lara	2002
4th	123	Mark Richardson & Nathan Astle (NZ)	2002
5th	143	Chris Gayle & Shiv Chanderpaul	2002
6th	99	Scott Styris & Robbie Hart(NZ)	2002
7th	48	Scott Styris & Craig McMillan (NZ)	2002
8th	56	Scott Styris & Robbie Hart (NZ)	2002
9th	49	Scott Styris & Shane Bond (NZ)	2002
10th	12	Scott Styris & Ian Butler (NZ)	2002

RESULTS AT NATIONAL CRICKET STADIUM

Date	Countries	Result
28/06/2002	v New Zealand	drawn

GUYANA

THE ONLY TERRITORY IN THE CARIBBEAN THAT is not an island, Guyana is located on the South American Continent. Guyana has a character all of its own.

In 1498, Christopher Columbus sighted the coast of Guyana while Sir Walter Raleigh was exploring the Orinoco River in his search for El Dorado — the still mythical city of gold.

The British arrived in the 1800s and by 1812, renamed it Guyana to replace the names of Longchamps by the French and Stabroek by the Dutch, who in 1616 were the first settlers.

The British retained control of the country until 1966 when it became independent. In 1970 Guyana became a Republic.

Located where the Caribbean meets South America on the North East shoulder, this most enchanting country boasts a city of some 400,000 people appropriately named Georgetown – the garden city of the Caribbean, a city which abounds with colonial architecture. Its botanical and zoological gardens are renowned, and standing outside of these gardens is a monument dedicated to the memory of slave rebellion built in 1793.

A giant seawall runs for some 300km along the Atlantic coast line of Guyana and protects the city, which is about 1.5 meters below the sea level. To compliment the sea wall, Guyana is also equipped with a series of canals that run throughout the city.

The wall has over the years become a meeting place for all Guyanese. For relief, the Guyanese can journey to the awe inspiring Kaiteur Falls or the Orinduik Falls and the huge Essequibo River.

Boasting a tropical/equatorial climate, hot and humid, with an average temperature of 28 degrees, Guyana can be quite hot, and the trade winds which blow on the afternoons are most welcome.

Guyana & Georgetown are a country and a town, that has seen the impact on a social culture of a declining economy. Georgetown night life offers its challenges and its limitations, but historically the Guyanese are perhaps the most hospitable people in the Caribbean.

The country's population is all but equally divided between the East Indians and those of African ancestry which, has over time, seen a rivalry for control of the political and economic well being of the country.

There are only a few hotels that could fall into the first class category and the restaurants are generally good, with a recent impact of the arrivals of Koreans.

It is almost safe to say that the Guyanese love of cricket will all but overwhelm the visitor and blur the overwhelming state of the obvious economic problems of a fine people – so from arrival at the Chedde Jagan Airport some 41km from Georgetown, to departure, one will enjoy the fine hospitality of the Guyanese.

BOURDA

This compact ground, newly refurbished, is circled by a moat and is home to the Georgetown Cricket Club which was founded in 1850, and was the first cricket club in the Caribbean.

Some 26 years later, 1884 to be exact, was the date that they moved their Headquarters to Bourda where the first match was played on the ground in December of that year.

In 1930, England played the first Test ever played on the ground. The match was won in fine style by West Indies, when they defeated England by 289 runs. This was the match in which George Headly scored 114 & 112 respectively (another immortal innings, to match his later immortality at Lord's) and where Clifford Roach made 209 in the first innings.

In 1968 Garry Sobers made 152 and 95 NO and lost three wickets in each innings, bowling a total of 68 overs in the match.

Quite expectedly many of the cricketing sons of Guyana have made their fair share of runs and completed great bowling performances. To be remembered is Clive Lloyd's 178 vs Australia in 1972/3 and Alvin Kallicharan's 101 NO on his debut vs New Zealand and Carl Hooper's 233 vs India in 2002.

The West Indies 1958 team, it will be recalled, made 317 for 2 against Pakistan in the fourth innings to win by eight wickets.

Bourda is subject to flooding, as with the city – the grounds lies 1.5 meters below sea level, hence the moat. For those visiting for the first time, it is well worth seeing the old photographs, to appreciate previously used wooden stands, and recollect the Members Pavilion between square and fine leg, and the Ladies Pavilion attached to the Members Pavilion which was built in 1912.

The Rohan Kanhai Stand was the most modern before the World Cup.

The Guyanese mound is not for the faint hearted as the DJs make no allowance for peace and quiet, blaring out loud music and complementing it with the continuous flow of Demerana Rum.

Stands abound and bear the names of the illustrious "Sons of Guyana" who have made their name in the Annals of World Cricket. Lance Gibbs Stand right of the media centre and the Clive Lloyd Stand are wonderful stands to watch from.

All of these stands allow the viewers to enjoy cricket, complemented by the hooting of horns, the banging of the cans, and the sheer exuberance of a people filled with the passion of the game.

That the passion and exuberance can sometimes be volatile and real, was evident in 1954, where the first riot at a Test match took place, when on the fourth day, the co-opted groundsman cum umpire – Badge Menzies, gave Cliford McWatt run out. The hail of bottles which followed this decision, forced Len Hutton to gather his England team to one corner of the ground. The tension was relieved when Johnny Wardle mimicked drunkenness and won some of the crowd over.

This first riot act, was repeated in 1972 when Clive Lloyd was run out (vs New Zealand) and when Alvin Kallicharan was given out LBW in 1977.

But it was in 1979 that things reached its peak, when in the Kerry Packer series, players decided the pitch was too wet to play, where upon the crowd invaded the Members Pavilion.

Nevertheless one has to search hard to find a ground with more atmosphere and energy. Perhaps, the Curry and Roti has a lot to do with the spirit in which the game is played. And those who now see some transformation and improvement to the facilities will, like myself, recall the many wooden stadiums on stilts, the uneven grounds and great atmosphere, as vendors roam the stands selling everything from bottles of rum, to beer, to nuts, to dark glasses.

STATISTICS

WIN/LOSS RECORD

Country	Played	Won	Drawn	Lost	Tie
Australia	7	4	1	2	-
West Indies	29	7	16	6	-
Pakistan	4	1	2	1	-
India	6	-	6	-	-
New Zealand	2	-	2	-	-
South Africa	1	-	1	-	-
England	9	1	4	4	-

HIGHEST INDIVIDUAL AGGREGATES
(West Indies Unless stated)

Player	Mat	Inn	NO	Runs	Ave	HS	50	100
Garry Sobers	7	12	3	853	94.78	152	1	5
Richie Richardson	6	8	0	766	95.75	194	2	3
Gordon Greenidge	7	12	2	621	62.10	120	5	1
Shiv Chanderpaul	6	8	2	555	92.50	140	2	3
Rohan Kanhai	7	11	0	551	50.09	150	4	1
Brian Lara	6	9	0	548	60.89	167	1	2
Carl Hooper	6	9	0	540	60.00	233	2	1
Desmond Haynes	7	11	2	531	59.00	111	3	2
Clive Lloyd	8	11	1	463	46.30	178	2	1
Clyde Walcott	6	9	1	432	54.00	145	1	2

TOP WICKET TAKERS
(West Indies Unless stated)

Player	Mat	Bll	Md	Runs	Wkt	Ave	BB	S/R
Lance Gibbs	6	1867	112	578	28	20.64	6/29	66.68
Curtly Ambrose	7	1332	66	469	24	19.54	4/37	55.50
Courtney Walsh	8	1604	61	623	20	31.15	3/25	80.20
Joel Garner	4	907	36	419	20	20.95	6/75	45.35
Garry Sobers	7	1680	95	577	20	28.85	3/20	84.00
Imran Khan (Pak)	2	487	8	319	14	22.79	7/80	34.79
Leary Constantine	2	627	38	199	13	15.31	5/87	48.23
Malcolm Marshall	3	504	10	247	11	22.45	4/110	45.82
John Snow (Eng)	1	258	2	142	10	14.20	6/60	25.80
Neil Hawke (Aus)	1	316	15	115	10	11.50	6/72	31.60

HIGHEST INDIVIDUAL SCORES
(West Indies Unless stated)

259	Glenn Turner (NZ)		1971-72
233	Carl Hooper	v	India 2001-02
209	Clifford Roach	v	England 1929-30
194	Richie Richardson	v	India 1988-89
188	Martin Crowe (NZ)		1984-85
185	Richie Richardson	v	New Zealand 1984-85
182	Terry Jarvis (NZ)		1971-72
182	Richie Richardson	v	Australia 1972-73
178	Clive Lloyd	v	Australia 1990-91
169	Len Hutton (Eng)		1953-54

BEST INDIVIDUAL BOWLING PERFORMANCES
(West Indies Unless stated)

22.2-11-44-7	Ian Johnson (Aus)		1954-55
26-7-50-7	Eric Hollies (Eng)		1934-35
22.4-2-80-7	Imran Khan (Pak)		1987-88
22.2-9-29-6	Lance Gibbs	v	Austrialia 1964-65
40-20-60-6	Lance Gibbs	v	England 1967-68
15.2-0-60-6	John Snow (Eng)		1967-68
32-8-72-6	Neil Hawke (Aus)		1964-65
27.2-10-75-6	Joel Garner	v	Australia 1983-84
30.2-8-90-6	Wes Hall	v	England 1959-60
67-34-113-6	Sonny Ramadhin	v	England 1953-54

HIGHEST PARTNERSHIPS (West Indies Unless stated)

Wkt	Runs	Batsmen	Match
1st	387	Glenn Turner & Terry Jarvis (NZ)	1971-1972
2nd	297	Desmond Haynes & Richie Richardson	1990-1991 v Australia
3rd	185	Daren Ganga & Brain Lara	2002-2003 v Australia
4th	251	Graeme Wood & Craig Serjeant (Aus)	1977-1978
5th	293	Carl Hooper & Shiv Chanderpaul	2001-2002 v India
6th	206	Inzamam-Ul-Haq & Abdul Razzaq (Pak)	1999-2000
7th	143	Martin Crowe & Ian Smith (NZ)	1984-1985
8th	120	Rahul Dravid & Sarandeep Singh (Ind)	2001-2002
9th	109	Tony Lock & Pat Pocock (Eng)	1967-1968
10th	97	Tom Hogan & Rodney Hogg (Aus)	1983-1984

RESULTS AT BOURDA

Date	Countries	Result
21/02/1930	v England	won by 289 runs
14/02/1935	v England	drawn
03/03/1948	v England	won by 7 wickets
11/03/1953	v India	drawn
24/02/1954	v England	lost by 9 wickets
26/04/1955	v Australia	lost by 8 wickets
13/03/1958	v Pakistan	won by 8 wickets
09/03/1960	v England	drawn
14/04/1965	v Australia	won by 212 runs
28/03/1968	v England	drawn
19/03/1971	v India	drawn
06/04/1972	v New Zealand	drawn
06/04/1973	v Australia	lost by 10 wickets
22/03/1974	v England	drawn
18/03/1977	v Pakistan	drawn
31/03/1978	v Australia	lost by 3 wickets
28/02/1981	v England	match cancelled
31/03/1983	v India	drawn
02/03/1984	v Australia	drawn
06/04/1985	v New Zealand	drawn
02/04/1988	v Pakistan	lost by 9 wickets
25/03/1989	v India	drawn
09/03/1990	v England	abandoned
23/03/1991	v Australia	won by 10 wickets
17/03/1994	v England	won by an innings and 44 runs
17/04/1997	v India	drawn
27/02/1998	v England	won by 242 runs
05/05/2000	v Pakistan	drawn
09/03/2001	v South Africa	drawn
11/04/2002	v India	drawn
10/04/2003	v Australia	lost by 9 wickets

JAMAICA

AS THE VISITOR TOUCHES DOWN AT EITHER
the Norman Manley Airport 16km from Kingston or
Sangster International Airport in Montego Bay, some 240km
from Kingston, he or she is instantly captivated by one of the
most beautiful places in the world.

This country of great sporting history and achievements in
all disciplines, home of the World 100m record holder Asafa
Powell and past Olympic gold medalists Herb McKenley,
Arthur Wint, Rhoden Les Laing and recently Veronica
Campbell and Sherone Simpson, is despite its small size, one
of the greatest sporting nations of the world.

Jamaica is also the home of the Reggae Boys, the first soccer
team from the English speaking Caribbean to qualify for a
World Cup birth; and the unmatched achievement of the
Bobsleigh team – not to mention the boasting of three
Boxing World Champions.

This country of 144 sq. miles boasts mountains, rivers,
streams, forests and areas of unparalleled beauty, also boasts
a cultural history unmatched by many. There is no denying
that the world has been awakened to the sounds of Reggae,
Ska, Dancehall and Mento, with its main exponents being
Bob Marley, Peter Tosh, Bunny Wailer and Jimmy Cliff to
name a few, and in the world of history (Marcus Garvey); and
in the world of religion, The Rastafarians.

The North Coast, with the towns of Montego Bay, Negril,
Falmouth and Ocho Rios, are diverse in style and substance,
and boast the finest examples of modern architecture blended

with Georgian designs. The World Heritage Town of Falmouth, (where the new Greenfields Staduim is located), stands as testimony to the blend of history and culture.

The North Coast offers all the amenities of a resort area, and all visitors must experience the likes of Dunns River Falls (Ocho Rios), Ricks Café (Negril) Doctors Cave (Montego Bay), Rose Hall and Annie Palmer (The White Witch) and in which area you will find the finest Golf Courses from the Rose Hall to the Tryall.

Driving from the North Coast, one will enjoy the beauty of Fern Gully (Ocho Rios), the historic beauty of Spanish Town (the old capital only a half hour from Kingston), not to mention the alternative route through Port Antonio, home of the Blue Lagoon, and Boston Bay, the original home of Jerk Pork & Chicken, and on through St. Thomas, home of Paul Bogle. Or the still other alternative route via Manchester, St. Elizabeth and Clarendon, where the beauty of the South Coast can be seen in Bamboo Grove, Treasure Beach, Milk River Spa (Higher Spa content than Boden Baden)and the main area for the export of bauxite and where the second oldest railway in the world still operates.

This island, the largest in the Caribbean and the largest of the English speaking countries, was the original home of the Arawaks, cousins to the Tainos.

The island was originally called Xayamaca (Arawak word) which means land of wood and water, and which was what it was when Columbus appeared on the island on the 4th May 1494 when he landed at Discovery Bay (Ocho Rios).

In 1509 St. Jago Le la Verge, Spanish Town was settled by the Spanish until 1655 when Sir William Penn captured the island for the British, making Jamaica a colony of Britain in 1660.

During the ensuing years the British used Port Royal as the base for its pirates until 1694 when the great earthquake destroyed the then wickedest city on earth, following which Kingston became the capital. Some 300 years later, Jamaica gained its independence on 6th August 1962.

Kingston, the capital of Jamaica, boasts a population with its neighbour St. Andrew of some 1 million plus people, situated on the plains of Liguanea which lie at the foot of the famed Blue Mountain (some 8000 ft. high).

This modern still emerging city with a few skyscrapers, is the cultural capital of the Caribbean, and Kingston, with its mix of modern architecture and Georgian buildings, boasts one of the finest National Galleries, and the Institute of Jamaica and the Arawak Museum, are proud repositories of the country's proud history. It is home to the world renowned National Dance Theatre Company and the Ward Theatre, which stands as a testimony to the past glory of Jamaica's Theatre works.

The city abounds with cultural parks and art shows and offers the widest array of restaurants.

A visit to Kings House, Jamaica House, Bob Marley Museum, Hope Zoo, the two Universities, UTEC and UWI, exposes the visitor to the seat of learning.

The visitor has choices of pubs, restaurants, bars and clubs and is as safe or unsafe as any city in the world where the traveler seeks his or her personal satisfaction.

Knutsford Boulevard in New Kingston matches the Hip Strip of Montego Bay in its offering of the real to the unreal and can be experienced on any night of the week.

SABINA PARK

Home of the Kingston Cricket Club since 1880, the grounds, like the early West Indies Cricket grounds, saw its first match in 1930 when England visited.

That first match made history, when England scored 849 (still the 3rd highest total in Test cricket), when Andy Sandham scored 325 and became the game's first triple centurion and Les Ames supported him with 149. The only high point in that innings for the West Indies was OC Scotts 5/266, as the smart & wily leg spinner laid his claim to glory. It is the same ground on which his son Al Scott made his debut.

With the West Indies limited to 286, England declared their second innings at 212/9. Facing a mammoth 836, the West Indies by the 9th day had made 408/5 with Headley making 223. Rain for the next two days interrupted the match, resulting in the English team halting its participation so that they could catch the boat home.

In 1983, at this ground, the West Indies recorded an extraordinary win, due to Andy Roberts fine burst of bowling, when with India on 164/6 and looking to draw, he took four wickets for one run. The West Indies were then set 172 to make in 26 overs, and reached their target with four balls to spare, due no doubt to Vivian Richards' 61 off 35 balls.

It was here that Sir Garfield Sobers made his 365 NO vs Pakistan in 1954 which surpassed Len Hutton's 364 vs Australia in 1938 at the Oval.

The lowest Test score on the grounds is India's 97, due possibly to the injury to some four Indian batsmen by the fiery fast bowling of Michael Holding.

On this ground, all the 3W's, Weekes, Walcott and Worrell,

have scored centuries, when in 1953 vs India, each scored centuries, Worrell 237, Weekes 108, and Walcott 118. In 1955 Australia scored 758/8 declared with five Australian batsmen scoring centuries: Colin McDonald 127, Neil Harvey 204, Keith Miller 109, Ron Archer 128 and Richie Benaud 121. In this match Clyde Walcott became an immortal with a century in each innings.

All of this was matched by Lawrence Rowe in 1972 when he scored 214 and 100 NO on his debut to Test cricket vs New Zealand. In this same match, Roy Fredericks made a brilliant 163 and for New Zealand Glen Turner scored 223 NO.

On the bowling side, Hines Johnson playing on his home field, took 10/96 in 1948, and Courtney Walsh 10/101 in 1989.

In 2004 Steve Harminson 7/12 is the most outstanding performance. The ground has the infamy of the only abandoned Test match (after 10.1 overs) when England struggling on 17/3 and with four batsmen being hit, appealed against the danger of the pitch, and it was allowed as it was considered too dangerous to proceed.

The modernization of Sabina Park which is now in place, is still complemented by the beautiful backdrop of the Blue Mountains at the Northern end. Like all West Indies grounds, Sabina hosts its own mound and it offers all that you expect from the partying crowd.

The George Headly stand is a true tribute to the man it is named after as it is here that you meet the true aficionado of the sport.

STATISTICS

WIN/LOSS RECORD

Country	Played	Won	Drawn	Lost	Tie
West Indies	40	21	13	6	-
Australia	9	3	3	3	-
England	14	3	6	5	-
New Zealand	2	-	1	1	
India	9	-	3	6	-
Zimbabwe	1	-	-	1	
Sri Lanka	1	-	-	1	
Pakistan	2	-	-	2	-
South Africa	1	-	-	1	
Bangladesh	1			1	

HIGHEST INDIVIDUAL AGGREGATES
(West Indies Unless stated)

Player	Mat	Inn	NO	Runs	Ave	HS	50	100
Garry Sobers	11	18	5	1354	104.15	365	4	5
Clyde Walcott	7	12	2	924	92.40	155	3	5
Brian Lara	10	16	1	922	61.47	213	6	2
Gordon Greenidge	9	16	2	794	56.71	127	4	2
Rohan Kanhai	9	14	1	755	58.08	158	3	2
Frank Worrell	7	12	1	604	54.91	237	3	1
Desmond Haynes	9	17	4	593	45.62	84	4	0
Everton Weekes	7	12	2	585	58.50	141	3	2
Roy Fredricks	6	1	1	580	58.00	163	3	1
Lawrence Rowe	4	7	2	567	113.40	214	1	3

TOP WICKET TAKERS
(West Indies Unless stated)

Player	Mat	Bll	Md	Runs	Wkt	Ave	BB	S/R
Courtney Walsh	11	2219	91	897	48	18.69	6/62	46.23
Wes Hall	5	1266	40	534	35	15.26	7/69	36.17
Malcolm Marshall	8	1417	45	603	31	19.45	5/51	45.71
Garry Sobers	11	2390	116	879	27	32.56	5/63	88.52
Michael Holding	5	986	34	475	24	19.79	5/56	41.08
Lance Gibbs	8	2510	131	858	24	35.75	4/85	104.58
Joel Garner	6	1153	42	503	22	22.86	3/22	52.41
Pedro Collins	3	585	13	334	16	20.88	6/53	36.56
Alf Valentine	4	1385	80	507	16	31.69	5/64	86.56
Kapil Dev (Ind)	2	483	15	224	15	14.93	6/84	32.20

HIGHEST INDIVIDUAL SCORES
(West Indies Unless stated)

365	Garry Sobers	v	Pakistan 1957-58
325	Andy Sandham (Eng)	v	1929-30
270	George Headley	v	England 1934-35
262	Dennis Amiss (Eng)	v	1973-74
260	Conrad Hunte	v	Pakistan 1957-58
237	Frank Worrell	v	India 1952-53
223	George Headley	v	England 1929-30
223	Glenn Turner (NZ)	v	1971-72
214	Lawrence Rowe	v	New Zealand 1971-72
213	Brian Lara	v	Australia 1998-99

BEST INDIVIDUAL BOWLING PERFORMANCES
(West Indies Unless stated)

12.3-8-12-7	Steve Harmison (Eng)		2003-4
16-7-34-7	Trevor Bailey (Eng)		1953-54
21-7-49-7	John Snow (Eng)		1967-68
16-2-57-7	Corey Collymore	v	Sri Lanka 2003
31.2-8-69-7	Wes Hall	v	England 1959-60
20.5-5-49-6	Wes Hall	v	India 1961-62
18-3-53-6	Pedro Collins	v	Bangladesh 2004
29-8-62-6	Courtney Walsh	v	India 1988-89
24-7-66-6	Kenny Benjamin	v	England 1993-94
33-7-84-6	Kapil Dev (Ind)		1988-89

HIGHEST PARTNERSHIPS (West Indies Unless stated)

Wkt	Runs	Batsmen	Match
1st	206	Michael Frederick & Lawrence Rowe	1973-1974 v England
2nd	446	Conrad Hunte & Garry Sobers	1957-1958 v Pakistan
3rd	295	Colin McDonald & Neil Harvey	1954-1955
4th	249	Andy Sandham & Les Ames (Eng)	1929-1930
5th	322	Brian Lara & Jimmy Adams	1998-1999 v Australia
6th	220	Glenn Turner & Ken Wadsworth (NZ)	1971-1972
7th	147	George Headley & Rolph Grant	1934-1935 v England
8th	148	Jimmy Adams & Franklyn Rose	1999-2000 v Zimbabwe
9th	122	Dilip Sardesai & Erapalli Prasanna (Ind)	1970-1971
10th	54	Stuart Carlisle & Henry Olonga (Zim)	1999-2000

RESULTS AT ANTIGUA RECREATION GROUND

Date	Countries	Result
03/04/1930	v England	drawn
14/03/1935	v England	won by an innings and 161 rums
27/03/1948	v England	won by 10 wickets
28/03/1953	v India	drawn
15/01/1954	v England	won by 140 runs
30/03/1954	v England	lost by 9 wickets
26/03/1955	v Australia	lost by 9 wickets
11/06/1955	v Australia	lost by an innings and 82 runs
26/02/1958	v Pakistan	won by an innings and 174 runs
17/02/1960	v England	drawn
07/03/1962	v India	won by an innings and 18 runs
13/04/1962	v India	won by 123 runs
03/03/1965	v Australia	won by 179 runs
08/02/1968	v England	drawn
18/02/1972	v India	drawn
16/02/1972	v New Zealand	drawn
16/02/1973	v Australia	drawn
16/02/1974	v England	drawn
21/04/1976	v India	won by 10 wickets
15/04/1977	v Pakistan	won by 140 runs
28/04/1978	v Australia	drawn
10/04/1981	v England	drawn
23/02/1983	v India	won by 4 wickets
28/04/1984	v Australia	won by 10 wickets
04/05/1985	v New Zealand	won by 10 wickets
21/02/1986	v England	won by 10 wickets
28/04/1989	v India	won by 7 wickets
24/02/1990	v England	won by 9 wickets
01/03/1991	v Australia	drawn
19/02/1994	v England	won by 8 wickets
29/04/1995	v Australia	lost by an innings and 53 runs
06/03/1997	v India	drawn
29/01/1998	v England	drawn
13/03/1999	v Australia	won by 10 wickets
24/03/2000	v Zimbabwe	won by 10 wickets
19/04/2001	v South Africa	won by 130 runs
18/05/2001	v India	won by 155 runs
27/06/2003	v Sri Lanka	won by 7 wickets
11/03/2004	v England	lost by 10 wickets
04/06/2004	v Bangladesh	won by an innings and 99 runs

GREENFIELDS, TRELAWNY

Situated on the North Coast in the picturesque parish of Trelawny, the new facility was built by funding from the Chinese (who may now take an interest in Cricket). Greenfields boasts all the modern amenities required to host the opening ceremony of the World Cup. It has a seating capacity of 25,000. No matches have yet been played.

Like everything new, its history is yours to be recorded, but in the meantime the visitor, local or overseas, will be able to draw on the history of Falmouth, the capital of the parish of Trelawny, where the first newspaper in Jamaica was published, and a city/town which boasts the finest Georgian architecture outside of the UK.

ST. KITTS & NEVIS

THE ISLAND OF ST. KITTS WAS FIRST INHAB- ited by Arawak and Carib Indians migrating through the Caribbean islands from South America 5000 to 7000 years ago. The natives established themselves in small communities and came to call the island Liamuiga, or "fertile land". This name most likely arose from the lush tropical vegetation and crops that must have grown around the central mountain in the island's rich volcanic soil. The island's central mountain peak is a 3792 ft. extinct volcano which now bears the island's former name.

In 1493, the Spanish explorer Christopher Columbus arrived to substantially occupied native communities, and staked a European claim. It was believed that Christopher Columbus gave St. Kitts and Nevis their European names, calling St. Kitts the island of St. Christopher after the patron saint of travellers. Although the origin of the St. Christopher name cannot be confirmed, it is accepted that it was British soldiers who shortened the name of St. Christopher to St. Kitts, its recognized name today.

When visiting St. Kitts, your on-island lodgings may vary widely - from private rental properties to lavish all-inclusive resorts - but no matter what you choose, you can rest assured that you'll never be far from a breathtaking view.

The consistently beautiful weather in St. Kitts and Nevis is just one great reason to go. No matter when you visit, you can expect pleasant temperatures and dazzling waters.

On the island of St. Kitts, every meal is a celebration. Decide which examples of the unforgettable local culinary style most tempt your palate and then prepare to embark on a tour of some of the island's best restaurants.

Seafood is extremely important to the island diet. Lobsters, crabs, sea urchin, and sea turtles are common delicacies, especially when paired with West Indian curries. Some popular main dishes are rikkita beef (beef marinated in champagne with Italian dressing), cookup (rice and peas with meat), salt fish, and roasted suckling pig.

WARNER PARK SPORTING COMPLEX

Warner Park Sporting Complex is an athletic facility in Basseterre, St. Kitts, St. Kitts and Nevis. It includes Warner

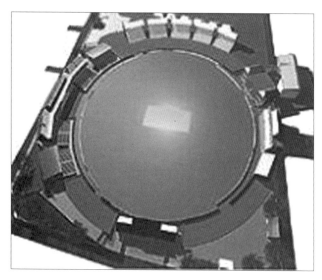

Park Stadium which has been rebuilt for the 2007 Cricket World Cup.

The stadium was largely funded by the Taiwanese government (they provided US$7.1 million of the total US$10 million cost) and built entirely by locals, while many of the other new stadiums across the region leant heavily on the Chinese.

It has a capacity of 8,000, although temporary seating for major events such as the World Cup can take it up to 10,000. No stands were built on the east side of the ground, allowing the prevailing easternly winds to have their cooling effect.

Warner Park staged the first ODI in May 2006 and its first Test a month later.

STATISTICS

WIN/LOSS RECORD

Country	Played	Won	Drawn	Lost	Tie
India	1	-	1	-	-

HIGHEST INDIVIDUAL AGGREGATES
(West Indies Unless stated)

Player	Mat	Inn	NO	Runs	Ave	HS	50	100
D. Ganga	1	2	1	201	201.00	135		1
VVS Laxman (Ind)	1	2	0	163	81.50	100		1
RR Sarwan	1	2	0	139	69.50	116		1
W Jaffer	1	2	0	114	57.00	60		0
S Chanderpaul	1	2	1	108	108.00	97		0
MN Samuels	1	2	0	107	53.50	87		0
V Sehwag	1	2	0	96	48.00	65		0
R Dravid	1	2	1	90	90.00	68		0
CH Gayle	1	2	0	86	43.00	83		0
MS Dhoni	1	2	0	49	24.50	29		0
A Kumble	1	1	0	43	43.00	43		0
Harbhajan Singh	1	1	1	38	inf	38		0
DJ Barvo	1	2	0	30	15.00	21		0
BC Lara	1	2	0	29	14.50	19		0
MM Patel	1	1	0	13	13.00	13		0
D Ramdin	1	2	1	11	11.00	8		0
Yuvraj Singh	1	2	1	8	8.00	8		0
JE Taylor	1	1	0	2	2.00	2		0
PT Collins	1	1	0	1	1.00	1		0

TOP WICKET TAKERS
(West Indies Unless stated)

Player	Mat	Bll	Md	Runs	Wkt	Ave	BB	S/R
Harbhajan Singh (Ind)	1	306	6	186	6	31.00		
PT Collins	1	285	5	183	4	45.75		
CD Collymore	1	240	7	103	4	25.75		
JE Taylor	1	222	4	158	4	39.50		
A Kumble (Ind)	1	354	8	200	3	66.66		
MM Patel (Ind)	1	234	4	177	3	59.00		
S Sreesanth (Ind)	1	222	9	118	3	39.33		
DJ Bravo	1	147	7	74	2	37.00		
V Sehwag (Ind)	1	96	3	47	1	47.00		

HIGHEST INDIVIDUAL SCORES
(West Indies Unless stated)

135	D Ganga	v	India 2006
116	RR Sarwan	v	India 2006
100	VVS Laxman (Ind)	v	2006

BEST INDIVIDUAL BOWLING PERFORMANCES
(West Indies Unless stated)

5/147	Harbhajan Singh (Ind)	v	India 2006

HIGHEST PARTNERSHIPS (West Indies Unless stated)

Wkt	Runs	Batsmen	Match
1st	143	CH Gayle & D Ganga	2006 v India
2nd	203	D Ganga & RR Sarwan	2006 v India
3rd	100	VVS Laxman & R Dravid (Ind)	2006
4th	30	MS Dhoni & R Dravid (Ind)	2006
5th	35	DJ Bravo & S Chanderpaul	2006 v India
6th	156	MN Samuels & S Chanderpaul	2006 v India
7th	77	VVS Laxman & A Kumble	2006
8th	14	A Kumble & Harbhajan Singh	2006
9th	5	PT Collins & S Chanderpaul	2006 v India
10th	47	MM Patel & Harbhajan Singh	2006

RESULTS AT WARNER PARK SPORTS COMPLEX

Date	Countries	Result
	India	Drawn

ST. LUCIA

THIS VOLCANIC ISLAND, LOCATED CLOSE TO
Martinique and St. Vincent, in the South East Caribbean,
forms part of what is called the Windward Islands. Only 967
sq. km., St. Lucia possesses great beaches, with fine coral
reefs and lush rain forests.

In 1500, Juan de La Casa, once a navigator for Columbus,
landed on the island and was followed by Francois le Clerc,
later to be known as (Wooden Leg), who settled on Pigeon
Island to continue his pirating ways by attacking Spanish Ships.

Over the ensuing years the fight for ownership between
the Dutch, who landed on the South of the island in 1600,
and the British, took many turns, and was followed by the
French who arrived in 1659. Between that year and 1814, the
ownership of the island changed fourteen times until the
treaty of Paris in 1814 left the island in the hands of the
British, where it remained until 1979 when on the 22nd
February it gained its independence.

The capital, Castries, colourful, clean and enchanting, boasts
somewhat noisy streets complemented by fine buildings like
the Cathedral of the Immaculate Conception built in 1897.

The Derek Walcott Square which leads in the centre of the
city is named after the noted 1992 Noble Prize Winner for
Literature, Derek Walcott.

The reported 400 year old Samaan Tree shades the whole
square and one can easily reach the Castries Market on the
corner of Peynier Street and Jeremie Streets, and offers a lively

dose of shopping and bargaining. A must is a visit to the Sulphur Springs.

The east side which is on the Atlantic side of the island, has a rugged coast line as against the west side which boasts the gentle Caribbean Sea. The fishing village of Anse-le- Ray is one way of entering and really seeing St. Lucian life. Within a short distance the visitor can experience the lush rain forests which boasts the country's wild orchids and tropical birds in all their magnificence.

Friday nights are known as 'Jump up Nights' in the village of Grosislet where Steel Bands, and other local music, compete with the fine stalls selling St. Lucian cuisine, all of which goes on into the wee hours of Saturday.

Thus it is from the arrival at Hewanerra International Airport located near Vieux Fort at the south of the island 63km from Castries. If one is flying in from neighbouring islands, one is likely to land at George Fl Charles Airport, just outside Castries on the Vigie Pennisila and is St. Lucia's regional Airport; which handles propeller flights from its close neighbours such as Trinidad, St. Vincent and Barbados, and is most handy for cricket fans.

A must see for the visitor is Soufriere, a small fishing village on the west coast and the first French settlement and where the Sulphur Springs are located. Here one can see and smell the bubbling pools of Sulphur bubbling water.

The Pitons, known as the two volcanic plugs near Soufriere, marks the Twin Peaks, which rise out of the sea to over 700 meters and over looks the village of Gros Piton.

Pigeon Island, this islet off the west coast holds a number of forts and a museum which hosts the history of the island from the Arawak and Carib's time to the French and British era.

BEAUSEJOUR STADIUM

The Beausejour Stadium lies north of the city between Rodney Bay and Gros Islet, and became a Test ground for the West Indies on the 20th June 2003.

Sri Lanka was the first Test cricketing nation to play here

and Marvin Atapttu had the first Test century, 118. Corey Colymores 5/66 is the first (bowler) to take five wickets; as Sri Lanka chalked up 354.

The West Indies then scored 477/9 with Brian Lara top scoring with 209 and Wavell Hinds chipping in with 113. For the Sri Lankans, Marahitharan took 5/138. The Sri Lankans then reached 126 without losing a wicket when time played its hand.

This ground, built in 2001, still has to build its history and will no doubt do so in the upcoming World series.

It is set at the foot of the hills, after which it is named, and up to this World Cup 2007, would be considered to be the finest stadium in the West Indies.

Built to hold 18000, its viewing facilities are excellent with its bucket seating and access for the disabled. The south side stands of Air Jamaica, Bounty Rum, and Harry Edwards, are good viewing areas, and the West end where the Julian and Charles stands lay on either side of the media centre, are themselves fine examples of modern comfort; here also can be found the Corporate stands, each with their own charm and excitement.

STATISTICS

WIN/LOSS RECORD

Country	Played	Won	Drawn	Lost	Tie
Sri Lanka	1	-	1	-	-
West Indies	1	-	2	-	-
Bangladesh	1	-	1	-	-

HIGHEST INDIVIDUAL AGGREGATES
(West Indies Unless stated)

Player	Mat	Inn	NO	Runs	Ave	HS	50	100
Brian Lara	2	2	0	262	131.00	209	1	1
Chris Gayle	2	3	1	234	117.00	141	1	1
Marvan Atapattu (SL)	1	2	1	168	168.00	118	1	1
Mohammad Rafique (Bang)	1	2	0	140	70.00	111	0	1
Habibul Bashar (Bang)	1	2	0	138	69.00	113	0	1

TOP WICKET TAKERS
(West Indies Unless stated)

Player	Mat	Bll	Md	Runs	Wkt	Ave	BB	S/R
Ramnesh Sarwan	2	288	17	101	7	14.43	4/37	41.14
Pedro Collins	1	267	13	125	5	25.00	4/83	53.40
Muttiah Muralitharan (SL)	1	300	10	138	5	27.60	5/138	60.00
Corey Collymore	1	192	5	74	5	14.80	5/66	38.40
Mushfiqur Rahman	1	190	8	90	4	22.50	4/65	47.50

HIGHEST INDIVIDUAL SCORES
(West Indies Unless stated)

209	Brian Lara	v	Sri Lanka 2003
141	Chris Gayle	v	Bangladesh 2004
118	Marvan Atapattu (SL)		2003
113	Wavell Hinds	v	Sri Lanka 2003
113	Habibul Bashar (Bang)		2004

BEST INDIVIDUAL BOWLING PERFORMANCES
(West Indies Unless stated)

29-5-66-5	Corey Collymore	v	Sri Lanka 2003
50-10-138-5	Muttiah Muralitharan (SL)		2003
20-9-37-4	Ramnesh Sarwan	v	Sri Lanka 2004
25.4-8-65-4	Mushfiqur Rahman (Bang)		2004
27.3-8.83-4	Pedro Collins		2004

HIGHEST PARTNERSHIPS (West Indies Unless stated)

Wkt	Runs	Batsmen	Match
1st	126	Marvan Atapattu & Habibul Bashar (Bang)	2002-2003
2nd	121	Javed Omar & Kumar Sangakarra (SL)	2003-2004
3rd	174	Wavell Hinds & Brian Lara	2002-2003 v Sri Lanka
4th	56	Rajin Saleh & Mohammed Ashraful (Bang)	2002-2003
5th	70	Chris Gayle & Dwayne Smith	2003-2004 v Bangladesh
6th	59	Chris Gayle & Ridley Jacobs	2003-2004 v Bangladesh
7th	136	Brian Lara & Omar Banks	2003-2004 v Bangladesh
8th	87	Mohammed Ashraful & Mohammad Rafique (Bang)	2003-2004
9th	74	Khaled Mashud & Tapash Baisya (Bang)	2003-2004
10th	46	Mohammad Rafique & Tareq Aziz (Bang)	2002-2003 v Sri Lanka

RESULTS AT ANTIGUA RECREATION GROUND

Date	Countries	Result
20/06/2003	v Sri Lanka	drawn
20/05/2004	v Bangladesh	drawn

ST. VINCENT & THE GRENADINES

KNOWN BY THE CARIBS AS HAIROUN ("LAND OF THE Blessed"), St. Vincent was first inhabited by the Ciboney, a grouping of Meso-Indians. The economy of these hunter-gatherers depended heavily on marine resources as well as land. They used basic tools and weapons and built rock shelters and semi-permanent villages.

Another indigenous group, the Arawaks, who entered the West Indies from Venezuela and moved gradually north and west along the islands, gradually displaced the Ciboney. They practiced a highly productive form of agriculture and had a more advanced social structure and material culture. The peace-loving Arawaks fished and collectively formed plots of land. The bountiful harvests and abundant fish, combined with the compact and stable island population, permitted the development of an elaborate political and social structure.

The first permanent settlers arrived on the shores of St. Vincent in 1635. These new inhabitants were African slaves who survived the sinking of the Dutch slave ship on which they were being transported. The escaped Africans merged with the Caribs and gradually adopted their language. Referred to as "Black Caribs," to differentiate them from the original "Yellow Caribs," the progeny of this group became the foundation of the Garifuna (which means "cassava eating people") who today populate Belize and Honduras. After several skirmishes both groups had agreed in 1700 to subdivide the island between themselves, the Yellow Caribs occupying the Leeward and the Black Caribs the Windward.

The capital city of Kingstown is located in the southwestern part of the island, hugging a mile-wide swath of land on Kingstown Bay backed up by a ring of green hills and ridges. Nicknamed the "City of Arches", Kingstown is full of old world charm, with Cobblestone sidewalks, old brick buildings and like many Caribbean capitals, much of the colour and bustle of the island can be found in the market square at the corner of Bay and Bedford Streets.

The city consists of twelve small blocks that are easy to walk and perfect for browsing. Shops and stores range from simple to sophisticated, selling local crafts, books, cameras, binoculars, watches, crystal and bone china, gold and silver jewellery, Sea Island cotton and batik.

In Calliaqua, check out Gourmet Food, they carry an excellent selection of imported cheeses, exotic meats and seafood, along with a good range other deli items. In the area you'll also find Howards' Marine who will handle your mechanical problems (they are the agents for OMC) and KP Marine, a general chandlery with an internet cafe, they are the sales and service agent for Yamaha engines and Apex inflatables.

On the other side of town, just across from Young Island, is an area known as Villa. This is where you'll find many of the island's hotels, restaurants and bars along with a few nice boutiques. When in the area be sure to check out At Basil's, a unique antique and furniture store, housed in an old colonial style building. They carry a wonderful selection of collectibles, home accessories and furnishings collected from around the world. Running the gamut from guest houses and self-catering apartments, to beachfront hotels and luxury all-inclusive resorts, accommodation in St. Vincent offers something for every taste and budget whether you are a honeymoon couple, vacationing with the family or on a business trip.

St. Vincent sports an eclectic range of dining options from beachside grills and take-away pizzas to simple, casual fare and more elaborate fine gourmet cuisine. Hotel restaurants are generally open to non-resident guests and further increase your choices. Along the Villa and Indian Bay strip is a delightful amalgam of local and international restaurants. Moorings around the Young Island Cut make many of these restaurants easily accessible to yachtsmen. For those seeking a slightly more adventurous lunch or dinner experience take the picturesque drive out to Pebbles in Mount Pleasant or take a boat ride over to Petit Byahaut or Young Island.

The area around Villa and Indian Bay is a popular tourist destination and many hotels are situated here. All the hotels are small and emphasize personal service. Kingstown itself has several hotels, while just outside town, in New Montrose, there are a number of hotels, apartments and guest houses. Venturing farther afield (and accessible only by boat) one finds the tranquil, eco-friendly resort at Petit Byahaut.

On the windward side of the island there are a number of beautiful black sand beaches. Especially popular is Argyle, a long beach unto which breakers crash furiously. Most of the windward beaches are not recommended for swimming. Also you will find a lovely picturesque long beach at Black Point.

Brighton Beach is a secluded black sand beach. This beach faces the Grenadines. It has high waves and is the perfect place for a bit of boogie boarding. Young Island Cut is a favourite with the yacht crowd. Anchor with care as the current sweeps both ways and the centre of the cut is 65 feet deep. Moorings are available, but stay clear of the sea bed close to Young Island itself. No customs clearance necessary.

<u>ARNOS VALE GROUND</u>

This ground has a capacity of 12,000 and a major renovation is underway as it will be a venue for warm-up matches for ICC World Cup 2007.

STATISTICS

WIN/LOSS RECORD

Country	Played	Won	Drawn	Lost	Tie
Sri Lanka	1	-	1	-	-

HIGHEST INDIVIDUAL AGGREGATES
(West Indies Unless stated)

Player	Mat	Inn	NO	Runs	Ave	HS	50	100
BC Lara	1	2	0	116	115	58.00		1
CL Hooper (SL)	1	2	0	115	81	57.50		0
PA DeSilva (SL)	1	2	0	113	78	56.50		0
ST Jayasuriya (SL)	1	2	0	107	90	53.50		0
A Ranatunga	1	2	1	85	72	85.00		0
RS Mahanama (SL)	1	2	0	57	29	28.50		0
SL Campbell	1	2	0	53	33	26.50		0
RIC Holder	1	2	0	50	34	25.00		0
SC Williams	1	2	0	46	46	23.00		0
CEL Ambrose	1	2	0	38	31	19.00		0
FL Reifer (SL)	1	2	0	18	18	9.00		0
MS Atapattu (SL)	1	2	0	17	10	8.50		0
HD Dharmasena (SL)	1	2	0	17	10	8.50		0
IR Bishop	1	2	0	11	11	5.50		0
RS Kaluwitharana (SL)	1	2	0	9	7	4.50		0
S Ranatunga (SL)	1	2	0	9	9	4.50		0
KSC DeSilva (SL)	1	2	2	5	4	inf		0
M Muralitharan (SL)	1	2	0	4	4	2.00		0
FA Rose	1	2	1	1	1	1.00		0
CA Walsh	1	2	1	1	1	1.00		0

TOP WICKET TAKERS
(West Indies Unless stated)

Player	Mat	Bll	Md	Runs	Wkt	Ave	BB	S/R
M Murlitharan (SL)	1	318	14	141	8	17.62		
KP Pushpakumara (SL)	1	190	3	122	7	17.42		
CA Walsh	1	276	5	135	6	22.50		
CL Hooper	1	136	8	47	5	9.40		
CEL Ambrose	1	144	2	85	3	28.33		
HD Dharmasena (SL)	1	192	4	88	3	29.33		
KSC DeSliva (SL)	1	180	3	108	2	54.00		
FA Rose	1	108	1	68	2	34.00		
IR Bishop	1	126	1	112	1	112.00		

HIGHEST INDIVIDUAL SCORES
(West Indies Unless stated)

115	BC Lara	v	Sri Lanka 1997

BEST INDIVIDUAL BOWLING PERFORMANCES
(West Indies Unless stated)

5/26	CL Hooper	v	Sri Lanka 1997
5/41	KR Pushpakumara (SL)	v	1997
5/113	M Muralitharan (SL)	v	1997

HIGHEST PARTNERSHIPS (West Indies Unless stated)

Wkt	Runs	Batsmen	Match
1st	62 62	RS Mahanama & ST Jayasuriya (SL) SL Campbel & SC Williams	1997 1997 v Sri Lanka
2nd		SC Williams & BC Lara	1997 v Sri Lanka
3rd		PA DeSliva & ST Jayasuriya (SL)	1997
4th		CL Hooper & BC Lara	1997 v Sri Lanka
5th		RIC Holder & CL Hooper	1997 v Sri Lanka
6th		IR Bishop & CL Hooper	1997 v Sri Lanka
7th		HD Dharmasena & A Ranatunga (SL)	1997
8th		CEL Amborse & RIC Holder	1997 v Sri Lanka
9th		FA Rose & CEL Ambrose	1997 v Sri Lanka
10th		M Muralitharan & KSC DeSilva (SL)	1997s

RESULTS AT ANTIGUA RECREATION GROUND

Date	Countries	Result
20/06/1997	Sri Lanka	Drawn

TRINIDAD & TOBAGO

SITUATED ON THE NORTH EAST COAST OF
Venezuela across the Gulf of Paria, this land mass was part
of the South American mainland, and indeed it is thought to
be the most Northern reach of the Andes Mountains. The
country, known to be volcanic in its origin, is on the south
end of the Caribbean chain, with the east of the island on the
Atlantic Ocean and the north west on the Caribbean Sea.
Tobago, the twin island, is some 21km from Trinidad, and
together they both host a population of some 1.3 million
people.

When Columbus happened on the islands in 1498 and
named it La Trinidad, he found the Caribs who had lived here
as descendants of the Amerindians since 6500BC.

The resistance of the Caribs, the only real warlike tribe of
the Amerindians, did not permit settlement until 1592 when
the Spanish founded the town of San Jose de Oruna, which
Sir Walter Raliegh destroyed in 1595. The Spanish then
moved to Conquaraba which they renamed Purto de Espana.
The British captured the island in 1797 and in 1802, under
the treaty of Amieno, it became British.

Tobago followed in 1814, and in 1888, the islands were
united as one country, remaining so until the 31st August
1962 when it gained independence and became a Republic on
1st August 1976.

PORT OF SPAIN

The city boasts a large Sea Port on the North West and is one of the finest cities in the Caribbean. The country, with its bellyful of oil, has shown remarkable growth in Architecture, Roads and Business. The city and the country is home to Carnival, and its cultural claim to Calypso and Kaiso is all but surpassed by the creative and interpretive origination of the Steel Band.

A bustling sprawling city, with Queens Park Savannah the axis, the Savannah has emanating from it, narrow streets which are very often lined with curb side food and merchandise stalls, overlooked by modern Skyscrapers which houses banks and financial institutions.

As one traverses the Savannah, with its horse racing on weekends, one passes the Red House in Woodford Square, home of Parliament.

The Botanical Garden is home to some of the Caribbean's finest flora. Two official residences, that of the President and the Prime Minister, are situated on the North side of the Savannah, as is the Emperor Valley Zoo.

The South side of the city hosts Fort George with its panoramic view of Port of Spain and the Northern mountains of Venzuela. Also worth visiting is Fort Piction, Fort Chacon.

From Carnival to Christmas, Trinidad and Tobago can boast a vibrant and colourful cultural heritage. The contributions of the different ethnic groups that settled in these islands have combined to create a rich inheritance in the realms of dance, music, art and cuisine, making Trinidad and Tobago a hot spot for culture in the Caribbean.

The two-day explosion of colour, pageantry and abandon that marks Carnival, Calypso and Soca music, our indigenous musical instrument the Steelpan, Chutney Music, East Indian Classical and Limbo Dancing, are all products of a dynamic heritage and vibrant people.

Many of the festivals celebrated in Trinidad and Tobago are religious in nature, including Hosay, Divali, Christmas, Eid-Ul-Fitr, Phagwa or Holi, Easter and Corpus Christi. Carnival may be the ultimate showcase for the plethora of artistic and cultural expressions in Trinidad and Tobago, but there are many other celebrations. Arrival Day, Emancipation Day and Shouter Baptist Liberation Day and several others, highlight the traditions and customs of specific ethnic and religious groups.

Tobago

Boasting the only white sand beaches of Trinidad, the North of the island Tobago has beautiful Bays (Kings Peter, Castura and Blood) to name three. The East side possesses Charlotteville, a fishing village, and diving and snorkeling will expose the visitor to marvelous reef, fish and corals, especially the Brain Coral. The main town Searborough is on the south coast.

Caroni Bird Sanctuary – In south Port of Spain this is the place to see the Scarlet Birds return to roost at sunset, and to witness this mass of bright red birds returning to their roost is most mind-bending and all to the accompanying sounds which will always echo in one's mind.

Tobago is the perfect place to relax in the embrace of lingering, golden sunsets. For the nature lover, Tobago is home to the oldest protected rainforest in the Western Hemisphere and, for those with an adventurous spirit, the waters surrounding the island hosts stunning coral reefs teeming with marine life.

Hilton – the upside down hotel.

Ferry – A ferry bus runs between Trinidad and Tobago and covers the journey in five hours.

Magnificent Seven – The name given to the row of eye impacting buildings on the western side of the Savannah.

Built in the 20th century, they are government buildings and worth viewing if not being able to visit.

Maracas Bay – Possibly the most popular beach in Trinidad. It lies some 30 minutes away from Port of Spain. The beach is good for surfing and swimming, and is one of the best places to try Shark and Baki, a local specialty.

QUEENS PARK OVAL

The Queens Park Oval is home to the Queens Park Cricket Club and is the largest Cricket ground in the West Indies, and has hosted more Test matches than any other ground in the Caribbean.

Nestled against the Northern Hills in the Woodbrook suburb of Port of Spain, the grounds saw its first Test match in that famous tour by England in 1930. The English tourists were victorious, beating the West Indies by 167 runs, with Patsy Hendren scoring 205-NO.

In 1970/71 Sunil Gavaskar scored 280, he also holds the enviable record of four centuries in five Test appearances there.

Everton Weekes remains the only batsman to score two double centuries in a Test at Queen Park Oval.

The 681/8 by the West Indies vs England in 1953/54 is the highest score on the ground. In contrast, England's 46 in 93/94 is the lowest. In that match, Curtley Ambrose 6/24 and Courtney Walsh 3/156, closed off the English innings in 19.1 overs.

Tony Grieg 13/156 has the best match figures and Curtley Ambrose with 66 wickets is the highest wicket taker; into the record books must also go Malcolm Marshall's 11/89 vs India in 1975.

In 1948 Andy Ganteaume scored 112 in his Test innings. India once held the World Record when they scored 406/4 to beat Clive Lloyd's team of 1975/76.

The ground, almost perfectly oval, is surrounded by some six stands, all well constructed and modern with further upgrading for World Cup.

Home of Brian Lara of whom the Trinis are most passionate, you can almost feel the pregnant air of expectancy when he is performing.

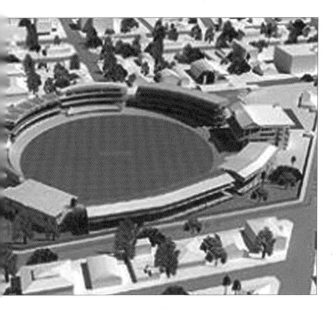

The Pavilion is behind the bowlers arm at the Southern end of the ground with the Jeffery Stollmeyer, DOS Santos and Learie Constantine stands come sweeping around the offside boundary, and are the most excellent positions for viewing.

Opposite the Pavilion beneath the high scoreboard is the Trini Posse Stand, a reserved stand which includes drinks in its admission fee all accompanied by calypso music, and the Carib Beer dancing girls. Definitely living up to its name as the 'Party' stand. The oval is only a five minute drive from the heart of Port of Spain, allowing one to arrive very quickly and so to share in the food offerings of Roti filled bread complimented by good rum, beer and mauby.

STATISTICS

WIN/LOSS RECORD

Country	Played	Won	Drawn	Lost	Tie
South Africa	1	1	-	-	-
Australia	12	4	5	3	-
West Indies	53	17	20	16	-
India	12	3	6	3	-
New Zealand	3	-	3	-	-
England	18	6	5	7	-
Pakistan	6	2	1	3	-
Zimbabwe	1	-	-	1	-

HIGHEST INDIVIDUAL AGGREGATES
(West Indies Unless stated)

Player	Mat	Inn	NO	Runs	Ave	HS	50	100
Rohan Kanhai	12	31	3	1212	43.29	153	4	4
Everton Weekes	14	13	2	1074	97.64	207	4	4
Clive Lloyd	13	28	2	1035	39.81	143	7	2
Viv Richards	8	21	0	1015	48.33	177	4	3
Alvin Kallicharran	17	21	2	982	51.68	158	3	4
Garry Sobers	9	31	4	954	35.33	132	4	1
Roy Fredericks	4	22	1	896	42.67	120	8	1
Desmond Haynes	7	21	3	801	44.50	143	6	1
Sunil Gavaskar	6	9	1	793	99.13	220	2	4
Brian Lara	4	22	1	786	37.43	122	5	1

TOP WICKET TAKERS
(West Indies Unless stated)

Player	Mat	Bll	Md	Runs	Wkt	Ave	BB	S/R
Curtly Ambrose	12	2770	142	877	66	13.29	6/24	41.97
Courtney Walsh	14	3345	147	1181	57	20.72	6/61	58.68
Lance Gibbs	13	4742	239	1646	52	31.65	6/108	91.19
Malcolm Marshall	8	2002	69	951	47	20.23	6/55	42.60
Garry Sobers	17	3859	181	1434	41	34.98	4/22	94.12
Joel Garner	9	2087	97	785	37	21.22	6/60	56.41
Angus Fraser (Eng)	4	1053	50	412	29	14.21	8/53	36.31
Inshan Ali	7	2686	106	1080	29	37.24	5/59	92.62
Andy Roberts	6	1352	41	670	26	25.77	5/56	52.00
Colin Croft	4	887	37	366	24	15.25	8/29	36.96

HIGHEST INDIVIDUAL SCORES
(West Indies Unless stated)

220	Sunil Gavaskar (Ind)		1970-71
207	Everton Weekes	v	India 1952-53
206	Everton Weekes	v	England 1953-54
206	Ricky Ponting (Aus)		2002-03
205	Patsy Hendren (Eng)		1929-30
201	Navjot Sidhu (Ind)		1996-97
189	Wazir Mohammad (Pak)		1957-58
177	Viv Richards	v	India 1975-76
174	Dennis Amiss (Eng)		1973-74
172	Polly Umrigar (Ind)		1961-62

BEST INDIVIDUAL BOWLING PERFORMANCES
(West Indies Unless stated)

49.4-16-95-9	Jack Noreiga	v	India 1970-71
18.5-7-2-8	Colin Coft	v	Pakistan 1976-77
16.1-2-53-8	Angus Fraser (Eng)		1997-98
36.1-10-86-8	Tony Greig (Eng)		1973-74
37.2-15-70-7	Bill Voce (Eng)		1929-30
66-15-162-7	Fergie Gupte		1952-53
10-1-24-6	Curtly Ambrose	v	England 1993-94
13-4-28-6	Vanburn Holder	v	Australia 1977-78
20-6-46-6	Charlie Griffith	v	Australia 1964-65
21.5-11-47-6	Glenn McGarth (Aus)		1994-95

HIGHEST PARTNERSHIPS (West Indies Unless stated)

Wkt	Runs	Batsmen	Match
1st	209	Geoff Boycott & Dennis Amiss (Eng)	1973-74
2nd	191	Colin Cowdrey & Ted Dexter (Eng)	1959-1960
3rd	338	Everton Weekes & Frank Worrell	1953-1954 v England
4th	237	Patsy Hendren & Lee Ames (Eng) Larry Gomes & Clive Lloyd	1929-1930 1982-1983 v India
5th	219	Everto Weekes & B H Pairaudeau	1952-1953 v India
6th	158	Gus Logie & Jeff Dujon	1983-1984 v Australia
7th	197	MJK Smith & Jim Parks (Eng)	1959-1960
8th	136	Bev Congdon & Bo Cunis (NZ)	1971-1972
9th	93	Polly Umrigar & Bapu Nadkarni (Ind)	1961-1962
10th	98	Frank Worrell & Wes Hall	1961-1962 v India

RESULTS AT ANTIGUA RECREATION GROUND

Date	Countries	Result
01/02/1930	v England	lost by 167 runs
24/01/1935	v England	won by 217 runs
11/02/1948	v England	drawn
21/01/1953	v India	drawn
19/02/1953	v India	drawn
17/03/1954	v England	drawn
11/04/1955	v Australia	drawn
05/02/1958	v Pakistan	won by 120 runs
26/03/1958	v Pakistan	lost by an innings and 1 run
28/01/1960	v England	lost by 256 runs
25/03/1960	v England	drawn
16/02/1962	v India	won by 10 wickets
04/04/1962	v India	won by 7 wickets
26/03/1965	v Australia	drawn
14/05/1965	v Australia	lost by 10 wickets
19/01/1968	v England	drawn
14/03/1968	v England	lost by 7 wickets
06/03/1971	v India	lost by 7 wickets
13/04/1971	v India	drawn
09/03/1972	v New Zealand	drawn
20/04/1972	v New Zealand	drawn
23/03/1973	v Australia	lost by 44 runs
21/04/1973	v Australia	drawn
02/02/1974	v England	won by 7 wickets
30/03/1974	v England	lost by 26 runs
24/03/1976	v India	drawn
07/04/1976	v India	lost by 6 wickets
04/03/1977	v Pakistan	won by 6 wickets
01/04/1977	v Pakistan	lost by 266 runs
03/03/1978	v Australia	won by an innings and 106 runs
15/04/1978	v Australia	won by 198 runs

13/02/1981	v England	won by an innings and 79 runs
11/03/1983	v India	drawn
16/03/1984	v Australia	drawn
29/03/1985	v New Zealand	drawn
07/03/1986	v England	won by 7 wickets
03/04/1986	v England	won by 10 wickets
14/04/1988	v Pakistan	drawn
15/04/1989	v India	won by 217 runs
23/03/1990	v England	drawn
05/04/1991	v Australia	drawn
16/04/1993	v Pakistan	won by 204 runs
25/03/1994	v England	won by 147 runs
21/04/1995	v Australia	won by 9 wickets
14/03/1997	v India	drawn
05/02/1998	v England	won by 3 wickets
13/02/1998	v England	won by 3 wickets
05/03/1999	v Australia	lost by 312 runs
16/03/2000	v Zimbabwe	won by 35 runs
17/03/2001	v South Africa	lost by 69 runs
19/04/2002	v India	lost by 37 runs
19/04/2003	v Australia	lost by 118 runs
19/03/2004	v England	lost by 7 wickets